Everyman Street

Everyman Street

Julian Colton

Smoke
STACK
BOOKS

Published 2009 by
Smokestack Books
PO Box 408, Middlesbrough TS5 6WA
e-mail : info@smokestack-books.co.uk
www.smokestack-books.co.uk

Everyman Street
Julian Colton
Cover photo:
Author photograph by Fiona Colton

Printed by
EPW Print & Design Ltd

ISBN 978-0-9554028-8-3
Smokestack Books gratefully
acknowledges the support of
Arts Council England

ARTS COUNCIL
ENGLAND

Smokestack Books is
represented by Inpress Ltd
www.inpressbooks.co.uk

for Fiona, Velvet, Rosie and Flora

Contents

No. 2: The Corner Shop

Anwar sits on the pavement exhausted
His back to the plate glass front window.
He sweats, swigs orange juice from a bottle.
Wears traditional white muslin, thick black beard
A hint of fundamentalism and Pakistan cricket.

He thinks again about his father:
First generation bus driving days in Manchester
Enduring the name calling and Paki bashing
Dog shit and fireworks through the letterbox nights.
Would Dad be proud of him?

Anwar watches the sun set over distant hills
His new neighbours return from weekends away
Disposable income caravans by the coast with husbands and wives
Dysfunctional fathers and mothers, dissatisfied lovers
Eyes them taking travel bags in and out of the houses.

The shop renovation is incomplete.
He wonders about the broken window.
Was it done deliberately?
Should he leave it until after the grand opening on Tuesday?

But the imperishable stock is in -
Coke tins, beans, margarine, coffee and toilet rolls.
The dream is taking shape.

A feeling of well-being washes over him.
It doesn't strike him as unusual,
When the various neighbours pass
View him sitting there on his haunches
Beneath the loud green convenience store sign,
Not a single hand raised in friendly greeting.

No. 3: A Poet

Except for the hand of the liberal poet.
Back from tutoring a course in deepest Devon -
The contemporary value of Karl Marx in fiction.

He carefully parks the blue *Volvo*
Walks over to the new store owner and introduces himself .

Harry Johnson's hands are pudgy and clammy
Round specs, bald head, green parka jacket.
He talks a lot, is jolly and friendly.

Anwar ponders whether he is being patronised
Need any help, you know where to find me.
Is confused by the poet's choice of profession.
Surely no one can make a decent living this way?

Anwar offers him a job serving in the shop.
At a very reasonable rate.
Four pound an hour.

Even Marxist poets have a price.

No. 10: The Policeman's Wife

Sarah Wilson averts her face
Passing in her new red *Mini*.

Anwar recognises that disdainful expression
Brings to mind soured cream.

She finally relents
Head twists to quickly consider him.

Those sea blue eyes
Tell of the distaste and sexual attraction
Of English women for Asian men.

He notes her cute, blue jeaned arse
Her Policeman husband's kissed greeting in the doorway.

His wife Jasminder inside watching *Eastenders* on television.

No. 15a: The Music Teacher

Only the piano can sooth Donald McGregor's anger.

Plays Beethoven's *Fur Elise* with overgrown, muscular hands
Arms honed by years of pushing the wheelchair
The 'spaz chariot' as the kids call it at school.

Thought he might finally tempt Laura in for a drink
But, as usual, she politely declined
Quietly took a lift from the unremarkable George
George with his ordinary head, legs and arms.

Fuck's sake! George is just a geography teacher
Not one decent opinion
His hands can't weave musical magic like this
Put pen to paper, compose a song.

Is one small drink too much to ask?
Does she think he's going to take advantage?
All he wants is some female company.

Granted, one thing can lead to another
Like his fantasy of taking her in the music store.
Does it matter she's seventeen and he's thirty-three?

Donald gazes around the ramshackle room
It could do with a woman's touch
Somebody like his mother in Australia.

He stops playing, pulls on a cigarette
Sees his face in the fireside mirror.
He hasn't shaved properly for days.

Rage rises in his stomach
Music sheets and metronome fly.

No. 15b: A Bed-time Story

Marian and Elliot Brown lie in bed terrified.
Wedged between them their son Robert
Wide-eyed with wonder, fear and awe.

Against the wall a cacophony of smashing objects
The Old English sheepdog's muffled barks
As below, Donald takes his living room apart.

No. 12: Bible Classes

This the biggest house in the street.
A meeting room for Bible classes
Beds for missionary folk
From America, Germany and France.

An understated air of religious conviction:
Flowing chestnut hair and doll like features
Beautiful Gina targets the men.
Muscular James recruits youth and women.

Both wear T shirts with mildly ironic slogans -
Jesus Saves and *The Hand of God*
Jesus in goal leaps toward a global football
Neatly timed for the next world cup.

But how do their own kids feel
Pushed from jamboree to conference?
Not allowed to play with the local heathens
Are they storing up slow burner resentment?

Made to attend Church on every Sunday
Smile at brethren whom they secretly loathe.
In the world of James and Gina – everything certain.
Their mission to recruit - ruthlessly efficient.

So what chewed at the heart and soul of Gina
Made her contemplate throwing it all in the air?

He was a Polish student from Cracow.
Arrived on a cultural exchange
Thin, pasty faced with a shock of red hair
The middle aged congregation called him 'Boniek'
In their seemingly impromptu kick-abouts.

James never suspected
Too busy flirting with the teenage girls
To notice her immediate attraction
To his honesty and cynicism.

Jan had the gall to say he didn't believe in God
Only came for a free holiday
Half the Polish boys did, apparently

Hoped to stay and find a job
In this land of milk and honey -
Wages four times as high as Poland.
You couldn't blame Jan if he lied.

Transpired he was a philosophy student:
Tell me Gina, how you get round the problem of evil?
Laughed at her reply that it was a question of faith
Ah, you move the goalposts.

Though her nipples stood on end as she masturbated
She never slept with him.
He'd touched somewhere far more deeply
Made her question her religious belief .

When Jan left she fretted for week after week.
One night in bed James finally tried to instigate sex
I can't James, she said, then told him she no longer believed.

He gently cradled her head:
Don't worry darling,
We'll get through this together.
It's just another of God's tests.

No. 2: Tariq Ali

Anwar's wife, Jasminder, half Scottish, half Pakistani
Made reconnaissance trips comparing prices.

Locals accustomed to shopping in the store
Time for the bargains to slowly rise.

A perfectly legitimate practice
He'd still be more competitive
Than the ubiquitous Tariq Ali
Standing before the counter in summer mode –
Flip flops, shorts, left and right chav heavies.
Made a good start, Anwar. Congratulations.

Anwar returns the smile
Grips the revolver in his jacket pocket.

The value of this store has surely risen
But you're becoming bad for business
Francesco - the ice cream and chip shop Italian –
Said as much yesterday.
Name your price, all is forgiven.
You can even stay in the house, work for me.

The smashed window now had meaning
A warning like the one his cousin received in Blackburn.

I prefer to work for myself, keep you on your toes
Ali's smile disappears, nose out of joint - he goes.

What did he want? asks Jasminder.
Wondered if I wished to join the Rotary.

But standing alone in the store
Anwar's face is thoughtful, pensive.

If he didn't have to worry about Jasminder and Yousif
He'd call up Johnny and the Moss Side posse.

This would take a more subtle strategy.

No. 7: Handy Andy

Forget the discreet tattoo and golden earring
Conspicuous party toke, chewing gum insouciance
The trendily shaved head and trainers
He's Neighbourhood Watch, community council
Masons, Royal British Legion -
Andy Mackenzie the local politician.

In the car it's Bob Dylan, Neil Young and Led Zeppelin
In chambers, the appropriate gear for every official occasion
The return of long lost town artefact
The personally commissioned Lowryesque portrait.

Named in gold letters on the honours board
The same man in every town across the nation.
Populace bends to an unyielding will
The pretence of liberalism
Pluralism, equal opportunity
His traditional status quo opinions
Supported by minutiae of AGM meetings.

Makes pacts with the devil to push business through
Smooths over conflicts of interest, especially his own
In the correct, politically correct manner
Despite skin as thick as a rhino's.

Knows whose calls to take and those to ignore
Which photo call enhances a 'Handy Andy' reputation
Or incubates petty jealousies, the wrath of grumpy men.
Has splinters in his arse from sitting on the fence.

Accepting Anwar's party contribution
Saves the shopkeeper having to attend council meetings.

Though Andy started with the best of intent
Does he really believe he can still change the world?

The Blind Pig Restaurant

Everyone links me to Conrad Huston
But he's not remotely the love of my life

Said Deborah Chisholm to Harry Johnson
60's sex kitten, 21st Century Greta Garbo
Julie Christie crossed with Jean Shrimpton.

It's all a question of collective perceptions.
I suppose the business sent me a little out of my mind.

Harry pours her another glass of house white
Imagine his excitement when she accepted his offer to dine.
He only wanted a brief interview for the literary mag
Called round on the off chance.
Deborah Chisholm - his childhood female icon.

Did it matter she was seventeen years older than him?
With the last face-lift she looked forty-three
But what the hell was she doing living on his street?
Jesus, she even bought her fags at Anwar's.
Standing in the queue, silk scarf around her once golden hair
Buying twenty *Benson's* with a Jack Russell.

I came for anonymity, nobody knows who I am
Here I'm Debbie Cartwright, my maiden name
I've got my dogs and cats and my studio for painting
Sell through an agent in Los Angeles.

Harry didn't care the article was out of the question
Proud she'd read his poems without prompting
Deduced she could trust him to respect her privacy.

The first time I saw you digging your garden
I couldn't believe it was you.
Hope you don't think this creepy
But I watched you discreetly from a distance.

Harry laughed loudly, the irony of her stalking him.
Who was he? A nobody in the scheme of things.
Bloody hell, it was so postmodern.

Then he remembered reports about reclusive behaviour
Days spent in the Home Counties sanatorium.

I'm alright now, she says.

Those beautiful trademark blue eyes pleading
At him, podgy, bald, divorced Harry Johnson
Minor poet, academic and scribe
A taste for very obscure world music.

He wondered if she craved the ordinary?

No. 10: Papa Francesco

A truism -
Sometimes in life you just get lucky.

On Tuesday, Sarah Wilson came in Anwar's shop for soup
        and matches.
Bingo! On Thursday he's in her bed in the saddle.
What a lovely face, what a gorgeous body.

She cuts his hair for free
Tells how her white cat is deaf
Sings to him in bed her cabaret act
And the unexpected bonus – Papa Francesco.

I call him Papa, but he's actually my Dad.
You see Italians are very Catholic
Though I've never wanted for anything
- the red Mini was a birthday present -
He doesn't officially acknowledge me.

As she talks Anwar's mind is in overdrive
Imagining potential scenarios.
Anwar knows the power of personal fantasy
Visualise and it can come true:

He is introduced to Francesco at a garden barbecue
The cunning Italian instantly likes him
Recognises a kindred outsider's soul
Realises here is a chance to undermine
That jumped up old bastard Tariq Ali
With his bad taste suits and pimping habits.
Competition is personal when it's closer to your age.

Anwar is useful, youthful, a potential protégé
Doesn't bother Francesco if Anwar's fucking Sarah
He did the same with her mother
Call it a vicarious form of absolution.

Anwar suggests a cut-price war:
If we call the shots
He won't know if he's coming or going
Then we slowly buy up his shops, independently
Fifty-fifty finance
I'll staff the stores, flog your ice cream and shit
And if he doesn't sell, that's his lookout.

Francesco smiles, bites on a sausage
That'll teach Ali not to run his own chippies
While his inward eye considers Anwar
Another contender, another dreamer.

No. 8: A Decent Man

Clive Sinclair feels like one of life's losers.

Started working life as a Yorkshire miner
Made redundant, became a Corby steelworker
Reinvented as a computer technician in the caring nineties
The shrinking Far East market did for him once again.

Sits at home watching daytime television
Walks the black mongrel dog, does the crossword
His headmistress wife calling the shots.

He'd like to have a secret vice
Be caught red-handed downloading Internet porn
As that unemployed bloke in the papers
Hit the bottle, take LSD, speed, meth, crack cocaine
Cruise the streets importuning prostitutes
Paid from an illegal bulging wallet
Laundered money in the bookies.
But he doesn't, he reads a lot of pulp fiction.
Clive Sinclair is a decent man.

He does the shopping and the washing
Puts all the clothes away neatly folded
Asks his wife's opinions
Takes her for a drink
Replaces the toilet seat
Only watches the football now and then
Changes the channels
Makes cups of tea, answers the phone
Kills all the spiders
Cuts the grass, tends the roses in neighbour's gardens
Was always nothing less than a considerate lover
Kind father to Clare away at university
How he misses her.

Clive Sinclair is a decent man
Sometimes he wonders if his wife really loves him.

Clive sees the sign on Anwar's window
Shop Assistant Required, Apply Within.

Mary Sinclair nearly swallows her teeth
Clive framed in the plate glass in the white grocery jacket
Packing a brown paper bag for a smiling customer
Anwar beside him, demonstrating how to work the till.

When Clive comes home
Mary gives him the silent treatment
Stares into space until -
Well, you could have told me.

You mean I should have asked your permission
You'd make some excuse why it wasn't appropriate
For a woman in your professional position
I'm tired of sitting around here doing nothing.

Mary Sinclair makes hasty enquiries
Learns that Anwar has had problems with the council
Something about plans for a chippy.
She thinks about moving out to the old schoolteacher's house
Attached to the rural school building.

In a pub conversation with the Director of Education
Seamlessly introduces the subject of divorce
- Referring to an unnamed colleague, of course -
It's clear separation is still frowned upon
Especially in relation to a small Church school.
She conveniently forgoes to mention
That she too has recently switched her denomination.

So instead of packing her bags, Mary is staying
She'll seek the advice of Gina and James at the next Bible reading
On how to end Clive's sudden, little rebellion.

But for now Clive Sinclair is happy
Tending to the whims of flirty housewives
The penny chew cheek of dirty faced kids
Daily entertainment of Anwar's bobbing and weaving.
Despite Mary's fears he's being corrupted
Clive Sinclair remains a decent man.

Cricket, Lovely Cricket

Anwar had always loved cricket
Believed in its mythical sanctity
An island of decency in an almost totally corrupt world
Where a sense of fair play could still prevail
Immune to the bounces of social vicissitude
If armed with a sword-like bat and a degree of talent.

On first showing at the club - welcomed with open arms
The secondhand *BMW* struck the right note
Four different bats hinted at Javed Miandad
The reverse swing bowling – Imran Khan.

Thirty wickets and four hundred runs in five matches
Conferred immediate lower league legend status
Slaps on the back, 30 quid slipped into his boots
'Annie' was a fondly accepted sobriquet.

The stats decreased with the impending opening of the store.
Dog-tired at seven o'clock on Tuesdays and Thursdays
He preferred a net with Sarah Wilson to practice.
Everyone noticed the quickly increasing girth
Rapidly diminishing pace and swing
An inability to read the softest of googlies.

Though he still scored runs and took wickets
He forgot the well-worn maxim –
In sport an outsider has to be outstanding.

His surprise one Friday morning
Name omitted from the high street team board.
For days he fumed, turned down the game for the seconds
Citing his need to prepare the shop's grand opening.

How could they prefer the undertaker's son to him?
A boy who never held a catch, took a wicket or scored a run
A trundling, bumbling nonentity.
This wasn't fair, this just wasn't cricket.
Anwar never showed his face at the club again.

No. 12: A Visitation

Gina listened for the post every morning
While James was shaving
She listened
As she dressed her youngest
She listened
As she sipped her tea…

Hoping that James would soon leave the house
So that when the letter fell onto the carpet
She is left alone to caress the bland Polish stamp
Read his carefully disguised words:

Poland is cold, I miss you all
It is hoped I will be coming over soon
Do you have email?

Gina did have email, but she also had guilt
A widely underestimated emotion.
She declined to reply to the four letters over six months
Yet inside, Gina yearned.

She didn't know what it was that she wanted
Easier if it was just a sexual thing
Like James playing around with teenage girls
Taking his pick of the forbidden fruit
Full of remorse yet making his selection again
A serial faller, but God his redeemer
Inspiring in him the best of intentions.
The making up was always thrilling, hot and fulfilling
At least until Jan came on the scene.

The best thing to do was ignore Jan altogether
The feeling of emptiness would pass
As memory of him inevitably faded.

Then one Monday morning, there he was at her door.
Hello Gina, I tell you I come.

Gina looked up and down the street
Like a lover in a kitchen-sink drama
Then quickly ushered him in.
The kids were at school, James at the Church hall.

What are you doing here?

I live here.

*You can't live with me Jan,
There's James and the Kids.*

Jan laughed loudly:
*No, you misunderstand
I live on Everyman Street. Number Thirteen.*

Transpires that Jan is sharing a house
Six Polish men crammed under one roof.
It is basic, but it is a place to stay.

The thought flashed through her mind
But she refrained from asking
She was too well brought up for such questions.

I have my own room. I'm comfortable.

But what will you do?

*Teach English to the Polish
The Rumanians and Portuguese
Until I find a proper job
Maybe in a supermarket
Or cleaning schools and pub tables.*

In Poland he was an intellectual
Had articles in many learned journals
Here the best he could hope for was a job for the lowest paid
But he wasn't bitter
If anything he was grateful.

How she admired his resilience
How he had kept his flame for her alive.
She couldn't imagine James smiling through such circumstance.

And then the truth hit her
Revealed itself like an epiphany
Minus the golden sun and angels.

She loved Jan.

The Bypass

George Wilson saw the car from half a mile away
A wide-angle panoramic shot, framed by his windscreen

Straight ahead on the opposite side of the road
A black ripple of silk metal in the dawn sun.

Veered almost imperceptibly like slow motion
A ship of death coming steadily toward him

The driver's white-haired head
Slumped on the steering wheel.

His Policeman's instincts kicked in:
Rammed hard to the left

Bumped ditch, sliced through hedge
Spun into field, rolled over and over

The bonnet split, prised open like a tin can
Metal and glass exploded, crumpled in his ears.

The Police car came to a halt, upright.
He'd survived.

For a full minute George sat still and thought of Sarah
Her clear blue eyes had worried him last night.

He twisted his aching whiplashed neck
The black car was fifty yards away

Nestled neatly between two tree trunks
Absurdly, as if purposely parked.

George strode over,
The car was barely scratched, immaculate.

There was nothing to be done
Probably a heart attack.

George breathed in the morning air
So this was how death came – unannounced

In the early hours with no one around
No fuss, no hullabaloo.

He took the man's ID from his coat pocket:
Pierre Levre, *en vacance.*

No. 2: A Close Shave

Anwar gazes at himself in the clouded bathroom mirror.
He is tired of this beard, this stance, this posture.
It is too much his past, he wants to move on.

Sarah complains it brings her out in a rash.
The scissors cut through thick strands of black.
Jasminder comes in and watches him shave:

You never go to the mosque these days
He shrugs: *I'm busy, Jasminder.*
She shrugs in return and leaves the room.

No. 1: Looking after Number One

Tyrone kept to himself at Number One.
Hardly left the house
Occasional stroll to the supermarket

To buy provisions, *Rizla* papers and tins
Milk and bread, a part-time flute playing musician
Straggly haired, tight filthy jeans, incredibly thin

Proud of his reclusive status
'I never bother anyone, man
Sitting in my haze of cannabis smoke'

Spoken to his brother on the phone
Still a prisoner to London life
Envious of Tyrone doing as he liked

Growing his own in the garden greenhouse
Selling it to friends on the Internet
To make a dubious kind of living.

Pushed by Anwar to adults – the occasional ounce
Live and let live Tyrone's liberal motto.
Not so the police who came one night

Smashed down his door
Dug up the floorboards, wrecked the place
Valued his crop at several thousand.

Community service deemed a small price to pay
Until Tyrone made a farting noise to the judge
On principle, said he'd much rather go to prison.

Today he sits in a cell with silent company
Doesn't make much sense
He now smokes dope at the taxpayer's expense.

No. 5: Sisters

Everybody assumed they were sisters
Short grey hair, sharp angular features.

Taught games at the High School
Former Great Britain hockey internationalists

Sharing the same surname - Carew
Changed by deed poll in 1972.

Products of Roedean
Clipped English rose accents

The window cleaner swore blind
Their bed was a double

But who cared
They never did anyone harm

The sisters were close
To each other steadfast and loyal

And he always had a dirty mind
Caught fingering the underwear of Debbie Chisholm

Swinging gaily from her washing line.
Life was a breeze for Alison and Chris

No men to dictate
No children to consider

Jogging together, sipping wine at night
Bit parts in the opera

Cruising the tennis club doubles
In white Billy Jean King type knickers.

Until along came Mr Alzheimer
Turned Chris into a total stranger.

Alison visits the nursing home twice a week
Patiently listens to Chris reprise

Bits of their own conversation
From swinging 1967.

No. 12: A Rude Awakening

The carousing in the street woke James

Luminous alarm clock – twenty past three in the morning
Parted the curtains a fraction
Sat on the edge of the disturbed bed
Peered into the streetlight orange.

It's those bloody Poles at Number Thirteen
Eight of them in a house
Piece of bloody nonsense

Gina roused, laughed at his pomposity
Such ungodly behaviour
Her irony flew over him.

He blustered about the kids being woken
But today his parking space taken
By a car with Polish number plates.

Those bloody Poles, Jan is one of them
She cajoled his sleepy memory
To recall the boy from Cracow
His scepticism, red hair and green eyes.

James remembers only the names of females
Has forgotten the kick-about with 'Boniek.'

A loud crash and laughs
The students retreat inside.

Perhaps we should ask them to the Church?
James rolls back into the warm bed
Considers her idea as he falls asleep.

Gina lies with her eyes wide open.

No. 3: Star

He should have known better
Once a star…
The trick had been making him feel wanted and needed
Flattering him about reading his poems.

She's never read a fucking poem in her life
Selfish, patronising bitches actresses
Think the world owes them a bleeding living.
Invective spat to his own image in the mirror.

Then he calmed
Realised vanity had made him vulnerable
The thought a famous beauty
Could fall for him on every level
Physical, spiritual, intellectual
A roly-poly, bald academic like Harry Johnson.

No denying the sex was the best ever
She aroused him in places he didn't know existed.
Pinewood and Hollywood – what finishing schools.
Her body still the body of a thirty year old
The flat stomach, round arse and firm nipples.

He concluded he got everything he deserved
She was right to ditch him
Being jealous about her old flames.
Christ, he was too old for the love business.

Now she wasn't returning his calls.
Two failed marriages
Time he learned life's harsh lesson -
He was better off alone.

So he picked up the phone
Left a message on her answering machine:
She was right, he was wrong
Hoped they could still be friends.

His life was becoming one of those trashy serials
He hated and deplored.

No. 9: Green-eyed Monster

What was it with men?
Why did they always turn into filthy, nasty pigs?
Wasn't it enough that she gave herself sexually?
Why must they totally possess her
Get rough, rude and physical?

Not one of them one was a real catch
Never mind plain Harry Johnson.
She sighed a sigh of true despair
Rubbed the blue bruise on her arm.

She had actually liked him
Relaxed by his clever talk and easy charm
Loved his poems, despite his misgivings.

Why couldn't he believe her reassurances?
She only went to London to visit her mother
Not to see the old cockney buffoon director
The one who still sent her flowers and chocolates
Cards with silly cryptic messages.

She knew more than most
The obstacle to love is possessive jealousy.

No. 10: A Homecoming

George Wilson discharged himself from hospital
Surgical collared aching neck
Blue-black bruise from shoulder to hip.

Declined the nurse's offer to phone his wife
Caught the bus home
Endured sniggering calls of boys on the back seats
Spying his uniform beneath his overcoat.

Limped up Everyman Street
Waved to Clive Sinclair in the shop window
With his own resigned 'things have changed' smile
Sticking up the latest offer
Francesco's Pizzas – three for two.

Opened the front door
Called out Sarah's name, no reply.

Hobbled and crawled upstairs
Heard their laughing noises
Between the crack of the bathroom door
Her lathered hands washing Anwar's brown chest
Singing softly, his head resting on her breasts
Smell of tea tree and lavender oils.

When did she ever sing like that for him
Warm, unguarded, natural?

He should have been consumed with rage
But felt a sense of relief.
He'd known for years the chemistry was wrong.

Sidled slowly back down the stairs
Spent the night at a female colleague's house
Came back the next day
Left a note saying
Sorry, hope you'll be happy.

No. 2: An Unexpected Delivery

A quiet Sunday evening
As quiet as Sundays used to be
Before twenty-four-hour shopping
The Internet and satellite TV.

Clive Sinclair watched Gina and James drive by
James at the wheel of the 'God Squad' jalopy
Crammed with teenage kids looking happy-clappy.
At least they were getting out reasoned Clive
Doing something social and vaguely useful.
Clive turned his attention back to the cryptic puzzle.

He didn't see the first blow coming
The bat strike the back of his knees.
He tried to yell and scream.
His vocal chords froze, seized
Warm blood flooded his mouth
As his nose burst open.

Jasminder heard the commotion from the upstairs lobby.
Locked the kids into the bedroom.
Crept downstairs to find Clive
Slumped behind the counter in a pool of blood and vomit.

The Police reckoned Clive got off lightly
Spent just two weeks in hospital
Questioned why no money was stolen.

Anwar made noises about installing CCTV
Suggested the attacks racially motivated
Told Jasminder the Police were ignorant and useless
He would man the shop with an armed heavy
His mind already halfway down the highway of revenge.

No. 15a: The Survivor

Donald McGregor is a survivor:
In a wheelchair from the age of seventeen
Car crash, the Melbourne freeway
Died five times on the operating table
Recovered, went to college, completed his music degree.

A hero in the Melbourne papers
He hated the able-bodied Aussie hypocrisy.

Desperate to make the most of life's reprieve
Upped sticks and left for London
Played piano and organ in West End musicals
Just to be near all the gorgeous showgirls
Felt like *The Phantom of the Opera*
When improper advances were shunned.

Though he had his fair share of love affairs
He never found the desired special one
Perhaps he was in the wrong profession
For women of loyalty and sexual constancy.
Thought they were always feeling sorry for him.

Changed his career to teaching
Moved to this town, this Everyman Street
Fitted in well in the local High School
He's been here now for five years.
In this time he's had one girl –
Dora Carter the thirty year old R.E. teacher.
Who didn't believe in sex before marriage.

In truth, Donald didn't really fancy her
His legs might be limp and useless
But Dora was the actual cripple
Heart shrivelled by an abusive father
She would never let herself go.

Lying alone on the bed beside her
Donald tried gentle persuasion – massaged her back
Caressed her thighs, even once kissed her breasts.
The blouse remained firmly buttoned
This paragon of virtuous ageing maidenhood
Was having no truck with 'smut.'

Even before the accident
Donald prone to temper tantrums
The musical mother's piano playing protégé
Liked to get his surly way.

Inside his frustration grew
Until one night on the settee in front of the telly
Turning down another clumsy attempt at intimacy
He punched her viciously in the face.

At school she hid the black eye with make-up
But that was the end of the relationship.

Donald didn't grieve
He'll keep trying to find someone new
Someone like seventeen year old pupil Laura
Yet to develop the sexual hang-ups of Dora.
Donald McGregor is a survivor.

No. 8: Straw

Beaten within an inch of his life
Clive Sinclair relished his time in hospital
A chance to get away from suffocating wife Mary.

Spent his days recuperating
Talking to refectory folk in his blue pyjamas
Sharing jokes and stories with the nurses.

Finally, reluctantly, ferried home by Mary
Instructed not to go anywhere near Anwar's in future.

Gina and James came round in a deputation
To gently persuade him into the fold.

Clive played dumb, smiled benignly
Pretended he'd give it some serious thought.

Deep inside his heels were dug in
He would be round to the store when his strength returned.

For six months he never left the house.

The final straw –
Gleefully told by Mary; Anwar had replaced him
With the problem boy from Number Four.

Mary came home late from a parents' evening
To find Clive swinging gently from the living room ceiling.

No. 15b: Ordinary People

The Browns at Fifteen b are ordinary people.

Go to bed and rise early
Don't smoke dope or take hard drugs
Elliot never beats his wife
Marian doesn't nag
Elliot is understanding
Rarely looks at other women
Son Robert enjoys school
Has no phobias or psychological problems.

They keep a fairly tidy house
She is down to five fags a day
He drinks four bottles of beer a week.
Holiday once a year in Lanzarote.

Elliot enjoys Internet shopping
Takes Robert to football on Saturday afternoon
Plays badly in Sunday league for *The Blue Magician.*
He is a refuse collector at the council
Takes lots of showers
Smells of cheap aftershave and deodorant .

Marian has a job at the newsagents
Cleans at the school, town hall and hospital
Does a Saturday at the out of town *Tesco*
Watches *Eastenders* and *Coronation Street.*
All this work keeps her figure trim
Only her skin hints at ancient poverties.

He drives a maroon *Skoda*
She an old, red *Fiesta* runabout.
Both complain there are not enough places on the street to park
He thinks of raising a petition
But quickly remembers his council position.

After ten years they still enjoy sex together, once a week
Kiss Robert goodnight after a bed-time story.
The Browns have no known ambitions
No frustrations, no hidden talents.

The Browns are the happiest people on Everyman Street.

No. 4: Blade

Anwar needed a little local muscle.

Luckily he had an eye for these matters
So soon noticed 'Blade' at Number Four
How young men gave him a wide berth
Went quiet when he came in the store
After midday and a night's casual bouncing.

Sarah told how he ran wild at school
The attempt at professional boxing
Lack of the necessary proper discipline
Football hooliganism and petty theft
His dinner lady mother's complaints about knife throwing
Pimpling the bedroom door with steel marks.

Asked in class his preferred profession
Blade's deadpan answer: *'a hitman.'*
Not one pupil had laughed
Remembering the .22 rifle in the alleyway, shooting cats.

A short, stocky five foot six
Blade made his name stabbing three gangsters in a pub.
Got off scot-free, his conscience never dwelled upon it
His young, childless eyes showed no fear
Not since his janitor father absented himself had he cried.

Installing Blade in the store
Anwar displaying a flashing neon sign:
KEEP OFF! KEEP OFF!

No. 12: Vanguard

James with Judy in the back of the 'God Squad' van.
Down a dark lane, James between her youthful legs
Promotes his own brand of evangelicalism.

Gina is aware, but God knows - she doesn't care
        anymore.

No. 13: Her Only Serious Lover

Gina's tentative knocks at the door
Drowned by music and laughter
The sound of youthful vitality.

Nobody came for a while
Until a quizzical female in spectacles
Ushered her into the cramped smoke filled room.

Five men and two females fell silent.
Posters of Kurt Cobain and Che Guevara.

Jan is taking a shower, he expects you
Haughty bespectacled reproach
Repressed male sniggers

The Polish girl softened
Perhaps you go upstairs, I bring both tea
Touched Gina's hand reassuringly:
Jan is a nice boy. Be good to him.

Climbing the steep, thinly carpeted stairs
Gina's mind flashed back twenty years -
Attending the lodgings of a young student.

Oh God, it was James
Her only serious lover ever.
An odd marriage – his computer, her history degree.

She and James had made love that day
She remembered the sound of rain beating slate roof
The Cocteau Twins and *Furniture* on the old stereo.

It wasn't raining today. Dull and overcast.
But she was resolved.

Opening the bedroom door
Jan rubbed his copper hair with a blue towel.

You are early. His neck reddened.
I put on a shirt.
She stopped his hand.

The room was small and pokey
Books, a computer on a table.

They undressed shyly
Pulled the bed sheet over.

Drinking the cold tea afterwards
She surprised herself by not crying.

No. 7: Retaliation

The brown envelope lay on the coffee table.

Andy Mackenzie groomed himself in the mirror
Recalled how Anwar placed it there innocuously
As if slapping a fiver on his shop counter.
Three thousand in cash was still a lot of money.

Apprehension rose in the pit of Andy's stomach.
Tariq Ali not an enemy to be made lightly.
Andy only accepted payment
Knowing half the cash was Papa Francesco's.

Francesco and Anwar a bigger sum total
Once Ali's proposed restaurant refused planning permission
By tonight's subcommittee in the Council Chambers.
Ali's establishments damned by association
The taint of suspect public health.

To cover the dusty snaking trail leading back to him
Was 'Handy Andy's' finest Machiavellian skill:
Prime an impressionable councillor with rumour
Another wishing to make himself a name.

Andy would argue, even vote, in the meeting for Ali
Then, in the pretence of preserving harmony, nattily abstain
Commiserate with Ali when next they met
Vowing to overturn this 'disgraceful decision.'

Andy wondered what to do with the money
Upgrade his wife's computer or buy himself a new car?

No. 2: Jasminder

To the public Jasminder was generally invisible.

Rarely served in the shop
Her realm - the upstairs flat
Swaddled in pink or purple sari
Attending her son Yousif's needs
Specialist sewing for the cousin in Paisley
Making Anwar's meals, cleaning and drinking tea.

To strangers a shock to hear her Scottish accent
Berating Anwar playfully when forgetting the stock
Chasing him down the outside stairs
To the store, his clearly defined territory.

Though in the flat she laid down the law
In bed she knew the shared moves, often on top
Too discreet to discuss private matters with other women
To her mind, phoney notions of sisterhood.
Jasminder – loyal, working class, Glaswegian Asian.

Anwar still enjoyed fucking her
Even after the baby arrived, the passion didn't die
If anything it was better.
Beneath the sari -
Lovely skin, voluptuous breasts and curves.

He never laid a finger on her or raised his voice
So much crap talked about arranged marriages.
Though she pondered his reasons for not going to the mosque
She and Anwar immensely happy
Both familes said so - Manchester and Glasgow.

So why did he start going with Sarah?
Because he was a man
Because he could.

No. 10: A Proposal of Marriage

It was never mentioned, not by Anwar.
He was too clever for that.

Did you ever hear of an Asian deserting his wife?
Said Sarah Wilson's best friend Carol in *The Blue Magician*
A raised eyebrow her rhetorical answer.

But Anwar had left it dangling
The mere possibility of marriage
A hint he might eventually leave Jasminder.

He'll never marry you Sarah, love
He's having his curry and eating it.

The Cemetery

In death as in life, Anwar felt like an outsider.

Strange, uneasy
At this, his first Christian funeral
A sensation approximating guilt
Watching Clive Sinclair's coffin lowering
Wood bumping, scraping the sides of the dark grave
Faces of aged relatives straining at the cords.

This was too mournful, too final
Surely death should be a kind of celebration?

He felt Mary Sinclair's eyes watching him
Accusing him – *this is all your fault.*

He should have given it a miss.

Come and you're an intruder
Stay away and you lack respect.

Clive was an employee so Anwar had to attend
He liked Clive and it was mutual
They talked about politics, football and cricket
More than with most standing around his grave.

From the back of his mind
Anwar dredged a half-remembered conversation:
Clive had said he preferred cremation
To a religious ballyhoo
Half the street standing in the pouring rain
Looking po-faced and serious
Wondering if *The Blue Magician* was open.

Poor Clive, dead and still subject to Mary's wishes.
All it needed was someone to read a poem.

It wasn't Harry reading Yeats or Larkin
Instead James recited some modern American crap
Hand in the air invoking his saviour
Jesus the redeemer saving poor lost souls
Old messages in trendy wine bar bottles.

Sarah slipped Anwar the screwed up paper
Smoothed it said – *We're through* in big red letters.
He saw from her expression she enjoyed this execution.
What was he anyway, but a surrogate father figure
For the permanently absent Papa Francesco?

He excused himself from the impending wake
Walked away unnoticed
Down his spine the old shiver of the neglected loner.

No. 8: The Wake

Surrounded by Mary's relatives eating Dundee cake
Gina and James sitting on a settee in silence.

How to tell her?
Should he stay silent?
He'd really done it this time
Judy swore it was a safe period.

How to tell him?
He'd never forgive her.
Adultery such a betrayal to the Christian male ego.
Notwithstanding his own hypocrisies
Crushing to be told Jan was the father.

They sip tea, remain silent

Watch family strangers reacquaint themselves
Geographically in time's relativities.

Mary in the kitchen crying
Consoled by Clare back from university.

Gina and James sitting on a settee in silence.
In their minds swims the word abortion.

No. 10: A Making Up

The text message took Anwar unawares:
cum rnd m lonli c u l8r Saz

The intensity of their passion a surprise too.
They were in bed the whole day
Doing it in every conceivable way -

Missionary conventional
In her mouth, up her arse
Her on top
Licking her clit, sucking his cock
Squeezing his nipples
Sweat dripping
Biting and scratching
Mouthing obscenities
Whispering tenderly.

Anwar never conceived he had so much semen
Hardly cared if Jasminder saw the marks.

Only when he left to go home, exhausted
Did he wonder if Sarah was having one for the road.

No. 9: Another Making Up

Harry Johnson standing in the pouring rain
Knocked again on Debbie Chisholm's door.

Finally she opened a crack

Saw the present and the bunch of pink carnations

Piss off Harry
I'm not in the mood for this shit.

Did he really think after all these years
Flowers and a present a unique selling point?
How many men had tried this tack?

She'd wavered a little with the batch of poems
Pushed through the letterbox a fortnight before
No denying he had a way with words.

His desperation had finally sealed his fate.
She was attracted initially to his aloofness
Now just another of the lusting, adoring multitude.

The more he begged forgiveness
The more she would despise him
Better if he totally ignored her.

Please! The flowers outstretched.

If you don't go Harry, I'm calling the police.

He dropped the flowers and trudged up the road
Clutching the present under his arm -
Two signed D.H. Lawrence first editions:
Women in Love and *Lady Chatterley's Lover.*

He was relieved when he reached home
Realising he still had the books
Knowing he hadn't given all his heart away.

No. 2: A New BMW

Like scrutinising a child for bad behaviour
Jasminder eyed it suspiciously from the top floor flat –

Tinted windows
Conservatively dark blue
Yet a disgusting piece of conspicuous consumption.

Anger rose in her chest
She ran down the outside stairs, into the shop

Anwar! How could you without consulting me?
Is this is your latest love nest?

She stopped, embarrassed
Seeing Andy Mackenzie handed his cigarettes by her husband.

What's the matter Jasminder?
Anwar irritated by this intrusion into his territory.
Luckily Mackenzie hadn't understood her accent.

She moderated, smiled
Have you bought a new car, Anwar?

Anwar doubly annoyed now
By her interruption of his business
The fact the car belonged to Mackenzie.

His political plaything had the new *BMW*
Anwar the older, crumbling model.

In a black Crombie overcoat
Mackenzie smiled as he passed Jasminder.

I don't like that man, Anwar.
He reminds me of a praying mantis.

No. 7:   An Old BMW

Anwar had thought to send out Blade
As the gang assembled outside Mackenzie's house.

Perhaps Mackenzie did need teaching a lesson
The car and the coat too much a feathered display.
Who knew where ambition might take him?

The first stone to the bodywork
Whooping laughter
Larger stones, bats, bricks and kicks
Rising to a crescendo of hysteria
As the windscreen shattered.

Mackenzie remained in the house
Had he called the police?
What would he say
Come quickly
Tariq Ali is punishing me for betrayal?

The car's torture continued unabated:
It's flesh torn with keys
Headlights poked out
In the streetlight half dark visibly crumpling
Losing consciousness, expiring.

The boys moonwalked across bonnet, roof and boot
Pissed all over it.

Yesterday the car was brand-new
Today a complete write-off. Dead.

The lynching party scattered like crows
Unashamed after their metallic garbage feasting.

Apprehension and then fear passed over Anwar
How long before Ali came directly for him?
Hurt one of his family?

He turned to Blade:
Have you ever killed a man?

Choir Practice

He found her because he finally stopped looking.

There coming together
A rare tenderness in Donald McGregor's life.

Her epilepsy compensated for his twisted legs
Evened the score in uneasy apologies
Women resisting the temptation in his company
To look at someone athletic and beautiful
Trying not to hurt his feelings. So dehumanising.

They were both cripples, equally fucked up.

At first he hated Chloe making a sexual beeline
Pushing his chair, ingratiating herself
Lowering her lovely pale tits into his vision
Then withdrawing, smiling from across the throng
Eyes searching for him above her choir book.

He had looked ridiculous over the schoolgirl Laura
Coming on to her at the Christmas disco
Wheelchair dancing, showing off.

He cringed at the memory
Trying to kiss her in the car park
Her shocked, girlish expression
It was all so horrible and demeaning.

Unprofessional, a betrayal of his position.

He vowed to keep to himself
Maintain celibacy and abstinence.

Within a week along came single mother Chloe.
Her daughter in his geography class
She invited him to choir practice at the parents' evening.

What made him love her was the fit.
Her leaving the rehearsal room in a daze
His finding her in the corridor, arms and legs and head
Thrashing like a wild bird caught in a trap.
Calming, slack muscled, spit plastered around her mouth.

Such a change to feel sorry for someone else
To consider not only his feelings
To put another before himself.

How could he not love her?

The Snooker Hall

Getting a gun is easy:

Blade walked into the snooker hall
Spoke briefly to a man who gave him door work
Left half an hour later with a rifle
Concealed in an oversized snooker cue box.

Killing a man is a different matter:

Blade toyed with the idea of using the knife
Slashing Ali's throat.
Too messy and Ali had protection
Both probably armed.

He would take out Ali from a distance
Like *The Day of the Jackal.*

Time for practice
Formulating the scenario:
He went into the woods, shot a few rabbits.
His cool eye still sharp.

He could shoot the wings off a butterfly.

No. 11: A Part-time Existence

Nobody in the street knew them.

Nor saw them move in, come and go at weekends
The grey anonymous couple in their sixties
With grey, anonymous clothes and car
Two retirement pensions, disposable incomes.

Where they came from - nobody asked
Where they were going – nobody cared.

Arrived every Friday night, left every Sunday evening
A twilight weekend life of no responsibility.
Voiceless folk with family elsewhere -
Manchester, Birmingham, Edinburgh, Leeds?

Since Mrs Blackwell died at Number Fifteen
Her house subsequently turned into flats
No eyes or wagging tongues
To give the street's fleeting folk roots.

In two years they would be bored
Sell the flat for a lard arse profit
Buy another cheap, rundown property, restore it....

We can't leave them nameless and faceless like this.
We'll call them Ann and Brian.
People would have said they were a nice couple
If they had ever got to know them.

Well, one Saturday night
While watching *Celebrity Fat Club*
Drinking a nice, ice cold beer
Brian had a heart attack.

Rushed to the local infirmary
Via strange, nameless roads
Where he knew nobody

Not the paramedics
None of the nurses
None of the doctors
None of the patients.

He had no idea what the rolling hills looked like
Beyond the white A and E walls
Would have no taste for the local food
Couldn't understand the mumbled dialect
Drifting in and out of consciousness
Wondering where Ann had gone

Not knowing she was making frantic phone calls
To panicked folk hundreds of miles away.

At four o'clock in the morning
Ann crying in the closed canteen, oblivious

As the hospital priest gave him his last rites
Not sure if he was Catholic

And his family sped up the motorway
In the lashing, friendless, freezing rain

He died.

No. 6: New Orders

Jock Brennan was ninety.
Needed help to blow out his birthday candles
Ten great-grandchildren vying to perform the ritual
At his extended family gathering.

Sometimes he felt guilty outliving two of his sons
Surviving hundreds of his comrades
Their names fading now in his memory
Though faces remained - young, vivid, fresh.

He thought of them daily, walking down the street
Dark varnished walking sticks
Burma Star worn proudly in his lapel
His neat tanned head still betraying Chindit fitness
The brown sugar eyes his state of nervous readiness.

The four night lights in his patch of front garden
Sensitive to the onset of darkness
He thought of representing his comrades eternal souls –
Buried in ground far to the East
Soft, yet undiminished by time.
Had they lived would they have forgiven
Their cruel Japanese camp guard tormentors?

For years he had hated and despised
Turned down requests to attend reconciliation meetings
Sure all the remaining 'boys' felt the same.
He would live out his life and die
But never, ever, forgive
The beatings, the deprivations, humiliations and killings.

His wife Jean understood
Cuddled him in the night when he screamed in his sleep
'Bastards!
His mouth jungle dry and spirit cracked.

But now Jean had died
He lived in his divorced daughter's house.
He could close the door at night and turn his back on the past
Save those four affirming lights in the garden.

The past came to his door
In the guise of the future:

Papa, I'm getting married
Said his youngest favourite granddaughter
The voice of feverish, youthful excitement
Yet to be compromised by betrayals and disappointments.

Looking up from his newspaper
Jock Brennan saw only the yellow skin and slanted eyes
Not the shy boy in baggy jeans and trainers
The floppy up-to-date hairstyle, hands in pockets.
Papa, this is Misha, we met at college.

No. 3: A Credible Female Character

Heartbreak hit Harry Johnson hard.
When his defence mechanism kicked in
He began to write
He always did at times of stress.

For once he discarded pen and paper
Wrote directly on to computer
But strangely, not love poems
Not in the conventional sense.

Before the break up with Debbie
He listened attentively to her professional complaints.
He'd thought of writing a collection
A poetic fiction, a versified soap
With a credible female character at its core.

Was this a subconscious love letter
To his estranged, idealised muse?

He'd written fiction before
A detective novel with women to the fore
But the savage feminist *Times* review slated:
Mr Johnson's female characterisation
Dwells firmly in the realm of archetype -
Maiden, goddess, wife, divorcee, mother, whore.

He would assiduously avoid this trap.
But how to create a strong woman without cliché
Parody of *Superwoman*, Superwomen or Lara Croft?

For the first time in Harry Johnson's writing life
He suffered chronic writer's block.

No. 3: A Perfect Moment

There was one perfect moment.

She was leaving his house after making love
She turned to him and smiled
Something about her eyes, her hair, her mouth
Said she was completely happy
Totally satisfied with him and her lot.

He wrote a quick poem about it in pen
Tried to recapture that fleeting moment of unison
When nothing else in the world mattered -
Good, evil, pain, famine, acts of God
Pushed to the background, briefly forgotten.

But it was a transitory beauty
And now it was gone.
Once again he scrunched up the paper
Put down the pen
Stared out of his rain lashed window

Would the perfect moment ever come again?

No. 12: Child's Play

Paul was a quiet boy
All the teachers said
Gina and James were proud
Loved him to death.

He was a likeable boy
Especially popular in the church Bible classes
Anxiously attending parishioners needs
At the weekend camps in the hills
The picnics by the river
He was just like his father they said.

He was a clever boy
Nobody saw him spit on Debbie Chisholm's car
On his way home from school.
Or the next day when he scratched it with a key.

The teachers wondering
Just who was the school's sneak thief?

The Warehouse Art Gallery:
Art for Art's Sake

Where to kill Ali? That was the question.
Blade felt like Macbeth toying with location:

The greyhound track at Gretna where Ali's dogs raced?
Too obvious and open.

The gym in town?
Down too many flights of stairs
Too many leotarded witnesses.

At one of Ali's business premises?
Anwar expressly ordered the killing to look personal
Not motivated by notions of the commercial.

A little chance research came up with the Warehouse -
An article in a local society mag
Twenty questions detailing Ali's 'favourite things':

Favourite food: *Indian.*
Star sign: *Scorpio.*
Favourite colour: *Gold.*
Car: *A black Audi A3. Smallish, but not difficult to park.*
What sheets are on your bed? *Four Hundred and Forty thread count Egyptian cotton.*
Favourite shop: *Harrods. One day I hope to buy it. Look out Mr Al Fayed.*
Favourite sports: *Football, boxing, greyhound racing.*
Football team: *Leeds United. I was born half a mile from Elland Road. I still have a few shares.*
Role models: *Muhammad Ali, Malcolm X, Casanova and Diego Maradona.*
Brand of underwear? *Calvin Klein.*
Ideal woman: *My wife or Nicole Kidman, Gwyneth Paltrow, Julia Roberts, Christina, J-Lo, Beyonce, Halle Berry...*
Lover or fighter? *Both.*

Favourite book: *The Kamasutra or Memoirs of a Geisha by Arthur Golden.*
Which magazines? *Four Four Two and Ring Magazine.*
Favourite group: *Queen.*
Wine or champagne? *Vintage Laurent Perrier, preferably pink.*
Favourite song: *Say a Little Prayer, Burt Bacharach.*
Oldest possession: *I have a very old copy of the Koran given to me by my Grandmother. A very wise book. I should read it more.*
One thing you wished you had known at eighteen: *Get out there and make deals. Nothing in life comes to you.*
Best kept secret: *Every Saturday morning I go to the* Warehouse Gallery. *They have a small collection of Rothkos. It is very therapeutic to sit there and contemplate. My best business ideas have come into being in the Warehouse. I also have some paintings and sculptures which I loan to the gallery.*

.

The Single Bullet Ripped Through Ali's Skull

Body jerked, slumped to the ground
Like a sack of slack coal
Before realisation hit his men.

Bodyguards frantically, aimlessly gazing around
From crouched positions, screaming fatuously, redundantly.

Majesty and its trappings are fleeting
Their King now dead
Long live the King.

Concealed on the roof of a disused hostelry
Blade made his getaway down a fire escape.

Bore hallmarks of a professional killing
Underwritten by a smorgasbord of jealous husbands
Choice of vindictive spurned women.

Ali had it coming.

No. 13: A Few Small Steps

Sometimes they made love so hard
Her legs felt full of water

Still feeling Jan rippling inside her
As she cooked the family tea

Her head distracted
She would forget to take a shower

To insist the kids did their homework
Revelling in the smell of Jan

The sweet sweat filled memory
Of pulling her arms up against the bedstead

Rolling with his crotch
Fighting the desire to come too soon

When he licked her, turned her onto her front
Fucked her from behind.

The disapproving looks of the Catholic Polish girl
Who now had a name - Sylvie

A small price to pay for such ecstasy
Such close proximity to physical divinity

But it couldn't go on forever
Everything has to come to an end

Especially when involving so much pleasure
And still to tell them about the baby

Both barely noticing her waist and ankles swelling.

The Church Hall: A Miscarriage

His first reaction was one of relief.
Then self-loathing, disgust
Fear Gina would find out
Throw him from the house
His kids field the hurtful comments of classmates
Their eyes accuse him of family betrayal
His status as hero, icon, role model – wiped out.

What of the reaction of the congregation?
Whispers behind hands
The moral outrage, losing his job.
He could leave the town
Would the Church help him relocate?
Was the concept of sin and redemption truly at its core?

After this he thought about Judy.

Listened silently, attentively to her telling:
Her lying in bed covered in blood
Crying, washing the sheets assiduously
The emptiness in her stomach
Feeling certain James would desert her now.

The Church Hall wasn't the right place to tell her.
The time - somewhere in the not too near future.

No. 2: A Unilateral Action

Anwar regretted his impulsiveness
The Ali family had glutinous tentacles

And Papa Francesco was less than pleased
By his acting alone, without consultation.

Anwar packed a protesting Jasminder off to Paisley
Are you in some kind of trouble?
No trouble, but just take Yousif.

He carried the gun in his belt
Under a big, baggy blue jumper
Safety catch on, mustn't blow off his testicles

Even though Sarah was doing that for him
Ignoring his calls, his playful texts
Clear she desired more than just sex:

I want normality, you in my bed at night
Want to cook for you, have your kids
Fucking isn't a proper relationship.

Given the stress, she was excess baggage
So he called her bluff and stopped phoning.
Hard to think of your dick when watching your back.

When Francesco came to the store with two massive men
Anwar feigned ignorance of the bloody deed
But knew Papa's lateral vision was eyeing up Blade

Standing guard by the door
Inside his coat, pocketknife primed.
Francesco took jelly babies for his grand kids

But this was a warning
An order to Anwar to draw his horns in
He didn't have Sarah to do his bidding.

He thought of asking Blade to take out Francesco.
A flight of fancy, yet Blade would be only too willing.
But Anwar wanted the killing to stop.

In his heart he knew the next tragedy was his
As Francesco had said, he was now on his own.

No. 13: A Routine Call

It was just a routine call
On an everyday Monday.

Sunday she and James had been at the church
Organising the youth, communing with the Lord
Projecting the image of a unified, believing family.

She had thought of Jan all morning
But James had taken an age to go to work
Something told her he wasn't himself.

Eventually she crossed the street quietly, unobtrusively
Anyone watching would think she was on church business.

Found the windows to the house all whitened up
The Polish girl Sylvie packing stuff into a van:
We're being evicted, someone else offered more rent.
As for Jan, yesterday he said it was time to be gone.

Something about a job in London
Just as well, you and he, the guilt was killing him.
Did you know his father was a priest?
There, you see, doesn't it explain a lot?

Gina nodded her head and walked slowly away.
James would be the father now.

No. 9: Meditations

She has slowed down the internal dialogue

Emptied everything out of her head:

The stage, films, husbands, lovers

The unsupportive parents, the seducers

The abusers, producers, directors, agents

Public relations, comebacks, falling ratings

Friends, enemies, casual acquaintance.

All are history, meaningless discarded entities

Like the once adopted fads and religions

The health spas and psychoanalysis

The suicide attempt and recovery

Alcoholism, abortion, sanatorium.

She has become herself – Debbie Chisholm

Revered international artist

A living island of one, with no room for anyone

Least of all - Harry Johnson.

She sits in her bedroom and hums.

No. 12: A New Testament

He felt like a disciple
Breaking open a bottle of wine.
Strangely, it was fish for tea.
He had sinned, repented
The child - a sign he'd been forgiven.

Tomorrow he would fish his Sea of Galilee
With a fresh perspective, a new beginning
Walk the kids to school
Wear a thick duffle coat and woollen jumper
Befitting a man in his middle-aged dotage.

He was made whole again.

Gina would keep up the pretence
Of the loving wife and mother
A shoulder for human parishioners to cry on

Her own life shattered into fragments.

The Bypass: Something Apocalyptic

(i)

Anwar had a natural suspicion of the police
Kept a safe distance
Never let their eyes meet in confrontation.

He was coming back into town in the early evening
Been to the cash-and-carry
Loaded the white van with weekend provisions.

Fucking a copper's wife was a stupid indiscretion
One sure to have repercussions.

Now the relationship was at an end
He'd waited for the female incrimination
The pointing of a vindictive finger
In an alcohol-filled conversation.
Anwar didn't realise PC George Wilson knew already.

George content to let it go by without acknowledgment
His marriage with Sarah through long before Anwar.
He was happy, seeing another woman
A traffic copper in the control room.

Only when the gung ho new boy from the Met
Sat beside him in the canteen did the ugly subject come up:

I hear that cocky Paki's been screwing your missus
That fucker wants teaching a lesson.

George insisted it wasn't important, he'd moved on.

Listen Bro' it's a matter of respect
This is our bleeding patch
He fucks with one, he fucks with us all.

(ii)

Anwar's van pulled to the side of the road
Dramatic flashing light, siren call.

He wound down his window, he'd play it cool:
What seems to be the trouble officer?
Too clichéd, laid back. The baton stick struck his head
Knocked him toward the passenger seat.

As blood gushed down Anwar's face
The ex-Met twat unbuckled his seat belt
Eased himself into the driving position

Drove the van off the bypass
Followed by two police cars, lights out, sirens quelled.
Into the smaller country road, put his foot down hard.

They drove for what seemed like an age
Anwar prostrate, semi-conscious
Wondering how he'd get out of this scrape.

(iii)

He could hear a dog barking, car doors slam
The sound of laughter, running feet.

Anwar was hauled from the van
In the dark, the dog bit his hand.
A boot kicked him in his private parts
Sent him to the ground
Took several more blows
Legs, head, liver, kidneys, heart
Then he passed out.

The View from Here

A loose piece of tarpaulin
Flapping incessantly in the wind brought him round
Cold blood freezing at his mouth
His shirtless body smeared in mud.

He quickly realised his predicament:
Strapped naked atop a church spire in the dawn
Leading player in the coppers' cautionary tale.

If he'd cleared his terrified thoughts to think
Would denomination have any symbolic meaning?

Perched on a narrow ledge two feet wide
His back attached to copper lightning conductor
By a thick, brown rope.
He was cold but secure
Wriggle his hands and he would soon free himself.

Looking down on his waking town, yes, *his* town
There was the bypass, the cricket ground
There the minarets of the mosque
He was overcome by a feeling of complete calm
Watching lights coming on in houses
Cars and vans revving their smoky greetings to the morning
Another day, one more disgruntled fresh start.

He tried to find Everyman Street
Wondering which landmark would make it stand out
Against the grey, amorphous mass of modern town plans?

Suddenly there it was –
The signage to his shop
Phosphorous green and yellow
Unreadable from this distance
But humming its silent affirmation:
ANWAR'S CONVENIENCE STORE.

He breathed in deeply
Thought of Jasminder and lovely Yousif
How she'd insisted he bought the sign
Thought about Sarah Wilson, Papa Francesco
Harry Johnson, Debbie Chisholm
Blade, Gina and James, Andy Mackenzie
Poor Clive Sinclair, Donald McGregor, the Browns
George Wilson, the Poles,
All those who come and go
The noisy louts congregating outside the shop, *his* shop.

All he could feel was happiness and pride.
It was so messy and confused
But it was real life, real death.

He had everything he needed.
He didn't want religion or politics
A modern economic system
A Church or police state
Or wished to be told what he couldn't do
Like the blindly obedient multitude.

The little kingdom he had created
He would continue to embrace it.

The Warehouse Gallery:
Debbie Chisholm's Street Tableau

What struck Harry Johnson
Looking at the painting in the exhibition -
The total absence of children.

Understandable, having no children of her own
He knew she'd had an abortion and thought of adoption
Did she feel a hollowness inside?

Flattered by his naked depiction - a lyre-playing Apollo.
She was to be commended for her powers of memory
His potbelly and thighs conveyed accurately, tenderly.

Though he recognised Anwar and others
Surely better for the odd cherub
A devilish imp or two in the clouds?

But again this was realism of a kind
For when did he ever see any kids on the street
Making a child's nuisance of themselves?

He remembered being chased off his street
By the coppers for playing football as a boy
The old Marxist laughed inside him:

Were they all indoors playing computer games
Watching television, doing revision
Transported to and from school in 4x4's?
Society reaps what it sows.

He felt old thinking in this vein
Placing a red dot by the canvas cheered him up.
He went home and played *Satisfaction* by The Rolling Stones.